GLUTEN FREE COOKBOOK FOR NEWLY DIAGNOSED

The Comprehensive Healthy Book Recipes to Prevent Diabetes and Satisfy your Taste Buds

CROWN GOLD

COPYRIGHT PAGE

Copyright 2023 by CROWN GOLD

All rights reserved. No part of this publication may be reproduced, distributed, or transmitted in any form or by any means, including photocopying, recording, or other electronic or mechanical methods, without the prior written permission of the publisher, except in the case of brief quotations embodied in critical reviews and certain other noncommercial uses permitted by copyright law.

TABLE OF CONTENTS

CHAPTER ONE 10
INTRODUCTION TO GLUTEN FREE DIABETIC COOK 10
CHAPTER 2 13
Breakfast Recipes: 13

   a. Gluten-Free Oatmeal with Fruit and Nuts 13

   b. Diabetic-Friendly Banana Pancakes 14

   c Frittata with Vegetables and Cheese: 16

   d) Gluten-Free Oatmeal with Berries and Nuts: 18

   e) Almond Flour Pancakes with Blueberries: 20

   f) Sweet Potato and Spinach Breakfast Hash: 22

g) Low-Carb Breakfast Burritos with Avocado: 23

CHAPTER 3 26
Appetizer and Snack Recipes 26

a. Gluten-Free and Diabetic-Friendly Hummus with Vegetables 26

b) slow-Cooked Beef Stew with Root Vegetables: 27

c) Baked Zucchini Fries with Homemade Ranch Dressing 30

d) Gluten-Free Baked Tortilla Chips with Salsa 32

e) Roasted Chickpeas with Herbs and Spices 34

f) Cheese Cucumber Bites 35

h) Sweet Potato and Kale Fritters: 37

CHAPTER 4 40
Main Dish Recipes: 40

    a. Grilled Chicken with Lemon and Herbs: 40

    b) Slow-Cooked Beef Stew with Root Vegetables: 42

    c) Shrimp Stir-Fry with Brown Rice and Vegetables 44

    d) Gluten-Free Quinoa and Black Bean Salad with Avocado Dressing 46

    e) Spicy Shrimp and Vegetable Stir-Fry with Brown Rice 48

    g) Baked Chicken Thighs with Lemon and Herbs: 50

Chapter 4 52
Side Dish Recipes: 52

a. Roasted Brussels Sprouts with Garlic and Parmesan....................52

b) Quinoa Pilaf with Roasted Vegetables and Chickpeas 53

c. Steamed Broccoli with Lemon and Almonds 55

g) Roasted Brussels Sprouts with Garlic and Parmesan:....................57

h) Grilled Asparagus with Lemon and Olive Oil:................................59

I) Creamy Mashed Cauliflower with Garlic and Herbs: 60

J) Steamed Broccoli with Lemon and Almonds: 62

CHAPTER 5 65

Dessert Recipes 65

a. Flourless Chocolate Cake with Fresh Berries 65

b) Gluten-Free and Diabetic-Friendly Apple Crisp 67

c) Coconut milk pudding with mango and toasted coconut 69

D) Smoked Salmon and Cream .. 71

E) One-Pot Mexican Cauliflower Rice with Beef: 72

F) Almond Flour Shortbread Cookies: 74

G) Low-Sugar Fruit and Yogurt Parfait 76

Conclusion: 78

Final Thoughts and Recommendations: 79

CHAPTER 6 81

30 DAYS MEAL PLAN 81

Day 1: 81

Day 2: 81

Day 3: 82

Day 4: 82
Day 5: 83
Day 6: 83
Day 7: 84
Day 8: 84
Dinner 84
Day 9: 85
Day 10: 85
Day 11: 86
Day 12: 86
Day 13: 86
Day 14: 87
Day 15: 87
Day 16: 88
Day 17: 88
Day 18: 89

Day 20: 90
Day 21: 90
Day 22: 91
Day 23: 91
Day 24: 91
Day 25: 92
Day 26: 92
Day 27: 93
Day 28: 93
Day 29: 94
Day 30: 94

CHAPTER ONE

INTRODUCTION TO GLUTEN FREE DIABETIC COOK

Understanding Gluten-Free and Diabetic Diets

Understanding Gluten-Free and Diabetic Diets and The Basics of Gluten-Free and Diabetic Cooking

When you have been newly diagnosed with diabetes and gluten intolerance, it can feel overwhelming to figure out what you can and cannot eat. Both diets require careful consideration of ingredients, portion sizes, and meal planning.

Gluten is a protein found in wheat, barley, and rye that can cause digestive issues for those with celiac disease or non-celiac gluten sensitivity. Diabetes is a condition that affects how your body processes glucose, a type of sugar found in foods. Managing blood sugar levels is essential for those with diabetes to prevent complications.

In this cookbook, we will explore the basics of gluten-free and diabetic cooking, and provide you with delicious and nutritious recipes to help you manage both conditions.

The Basics of Gluten-Free and Diabetic Cooking:

When following a gluten-free and diabetic diet, it is essential to focus on whole, nutrient-dense foods. These include fruits, vegetables, lean protein sources, and whole grains like quinoa and brown rice. Here are some tips for cooking and meal planning with these diets in mind:

- Read Labels Carefully: Avoid any products that contain gluten or added sugars, as these can cause spikes in blood sugar levels.
- Use Gluten-Free Flours: Instead of using wheat flour, try gluten-free flours such as almond flour or coconut flour, which can be used in many recipes.
- Choose Low-Glycemic Index Foods: These foods have a slower impact on blood sugar levels, helping to prevent spikes. Examples include sweet potatoes, quinoa, and berries.
- Incorporate Healthy Fats: Fats like avocados, nuts, and olive oil can help slow

the absorption of glucose into the bloodstream and promote satiety.
- Meal Plan and Prep: Planning ahead can help you stay on track and avoid unhealthy choices when hunger strikes. Try preparing meals and snacks in advance to save time during the week.
- By following these basic principles, you can create delicious and satisfying meals that support your health and well-being. Let's get cooking!

CHAPTER 2

BREAKFAST RECIPES:
A. GLUTEN-FREE OATMEAL WITH FRUIT AND NUTS

Here is a recipe for gluten-free oatmeal with fruit and nuts:

Ingredients:

- 1 cup gluten-free rolled oats
- 2 cups water
- 1/4 teaspoon salt
- 1/4 cup chopped nuts (such as almonds, walnuts, or pecans)
- 1/4 cup dried fruit (such as raisins, cranberries, or apricots)
- 1/2 cup fresh fruit (such as sliced bananas, strawberries, or blueberries)
- 1 tablespoon honey or maple syrup (optional)

Instructions:

1. In a medium-sized pot, bring 2 cups of water and 1/4 teaspoon of salt to a boil.
2. Add 1 cup of gluten-free rolled oats to the pot and reduce heat to a simmer.

3. Cook the oats for 5-7 minutes, stirring occasionally, until the oats have absorbed most of the water and are tender.
4. Once the oats are cooked, remove the pot from the heat and stir in the chopped nuts, dried fruit, and fresh fruit.
5. If desired, drizzle 1 tablespoon of honey or maple syrup over the top of the oatmeal.
6. Serve the oatmeal immediately and enjoy!

B. DIABETIC-FRIENDLY BANANA PANCAKES

Here's a recipe for diabetic-friendly banana pancakes:

Ingredients:

- 1 cup almond flour

- 1 tsp baking powder
- 1/4 tsp salt
- 1 ripe banana, mashed
- 2 eggs
- 1/4 cup unsweetened almond milk
- 1 tsp vanilla extract
- Coconut oil for cooking

Instructions:

1. In a medium bowl, whisk together almond flour, baking powder, and salt.
2. In a separate bowl, mash the ripe banana with a fork. Add eggs, almond milk, and vanilla extract to the banana and mix well.
3. Combine the wet and dry ingredients, mixing until just combined.
4. Heat a non-stick skillet over medium heat. Add a small amount of coconut oil to the pan.
5. Use a 1/4 cup measuring cup to scoop batter onto the skillet. Cook until the edges of the pancake begin to set and the surface is bubbly. Flip and cook for an additional 1-2 minutes on the other side.
6. Repeat with the remaining batter, adding more coconut oil to the pan as necessary.

7. Serve hot with your favorite toppings, such as fresh berries, sugar-free syrup, or a dollop of Greek yogurt.
8. Enjoy your delicious and diabetic-friendly banana pancakes!

C FRITTATA WITH VEGETABLES AND CHEESE:

Sure, here's a recipe for a delicious frittata with vegetables and cheese:

Ingredients:

- 6 large eggs
- 1/2 cup milk
- 1/2 teaspoon salt
- 1/4 teaspoon black pepper
- 1 tablespoon olive oil

- 1 small onion, diced
- 1 red bell pepper, diced
- 1 cup sliced mushrooms
- 1 cup baby spinach leaves
- 1/2 cup shredded cheddar cheese

Instructions:

1. Preheat your oven to 350°F (175°C).
2. In a medium mixing bowl, whisk together the eggs, milk, salt, and black pepper.
3. In a large oven-safe skillet, heat the olive oil over medium heat. Add the onion and red bell pepper and cook for 5 minutes until soft.
4. Add the mushrooms and cook for an additional 3 minutes.
5. Add the spinach and cook until it wilts, about 2 minutes.
6. Pour the egg mixture into the skillet and use a spatula to distribute the vegetables evenly.
7. Cook for about 5 minutes or until the edges start to set.
8. Sprinkle the shredded cheddar cheese over the top.
9. Transfer the skillet to the preheated oven and bake for 15-20 minutes or until the

frittata is set and the cheese is melted and bubbly.
10. Remove from the oven and let the frittata cool for a few minutes before slicing and serving.

11 Enjoy your delicious and nutritious frittata with vegetables and cheese

D)GLUTEN-FREE OATMEAL WITH BERRIES AND NUTS:

Sure, here is a recipe for gluten-free oatmeal with berries and nuts:

Ingredients:

- 1 cup gluten-free rolled oats
- 2 cups water

- 1/4 tsp salt
- 1/2 cup mixed berries (such as strawberries, blueberries, raspberries, or blackberries)
- 1/4 cup chopped nuts (such as almonds, pecans, or walnuts)
- Optional: milk or non-dairy milk, honey or maple syrup for sweetness

Instructions:

- In a medium-sized pot, combine the gluten-free rolled oats, water, and salt.
- Bring the mixture to a boil, then reduce the heat to low and let it simmer for 10-15 minutes or until the oats have absorbed most of the water and are soft.
- Once the oats are cooked, remove the pot from the heat and let it sit for 1-2 minutes.
- Divide the oatmeal into bowls and top each bowl with the mixed berries and chopped nuts.
- If desired, drizzle with honey or maple syrup and add a splash of milk or non-dairy milk.
- Your gluten-free oatmeal with berries and nuts is now ready to serve! Enjoy.

E) ALMOND FLOUR PANCAKES WITH BLUEBERRIES:

Here's a recipe for almond flour pancakes with blueberries:

Ingredients:

- 1 cup almond flour
- 2 tablespoons coconut flour
- 2 teaspoons baking powder
- 1/4 teaspoon salt
- 2 eggs
- 1/4 cup unsweetened almond milk (or milk of choice)
- 2 tablespoons maple syrup
- 1 teaspoon vanilla extract
- 1/2 cup fresh blueberries

- Coconut oil or butter, for cooking

Instructions:

1. In a large mixing bowl, combine the almond flour, coconut flour, baking powder, and salt. Stir well to combine.
2. In a separate mixing bowl, whisk together the eggs, almond milk, maple syrup, and vanilla extract until smooth.
3. Pour the wet mixture into the dry mixture and stir well until fully combined. The batter will be thick.
4. Gently fold in the blueberries, being careful not to overmix.
5. Heat a large skillet over medium heat and add a dollop of coconut oil or butter to grease the pan.
6. Once the pan is hot, scoop about 1/4 cup of batter onto the skillet for each pancake.
7. Cook for 2-3 minutes on each side or until golden brown and cooked through.
8. Serve the almond flour pancakes with additional blueberries and maple syrup, if desired.

9. Enjoy your delicious gluten-free and grain-free almond flour pancakes with blueberries!

F) SWEET POTATO AND SPINACH BREAKFAST HASH:

Here's a recipe for a delicious and nutritious Sweet Potato and Spinach Breakfast Hash:

Ingredients:

- 1 large sweet potato, peeled and diced into small cubes
- 2 tablespoons olive oil
- 1 small onion, chopped
- 2 cloves garlic, minced
- 2 cups fresh baby spinach
- 4 large eggs
- Salt and pepper, to taste

Instructions:

1. Heat the olive oil in a large skillet over medium heat. Add the chopped onion and minced garlic, and sauté until the onion is translucent, about 3-4 minutes.
2. Add the diced sweet potato to the skillet and stir to combine with the onion and garlic.

Cook for about 10 minutes, or until the sweet potato is tender and slightly browned.
3. Add the baby spinach to the skillet and stir until it is wilted and fully incorporated with the sweet potato mixture. Cook for an additional 2-3 minutes.
4. Use a spoon to create 4 wells in the sweet potato and spinach mixture, then crack an egg into each well.
5. Cover the skillet and cook for 5-8 minutes, or until the eggs are cooked to your liking.
6. Remove the skillet from heat and sprinkle salt and pepper over the top of the breakfast hash.
7. Serve hot and enjoy!
8. This sweet potato and spinach breakfast hash is a healthy and satisfying way to start your day!

G) LOW-CARB BREAKFAST BURRITOS WITH AVOCADO:

Here's a recipe for a delicious and low-carb breakfast burrito with avocado:

Ingredients:

- 4 large eggs

- 2 tablespoons milk or unsweetened almond milk
- Salt and pepper, to taste
- 1 tablespoon butter or coconut oil
- 4 low-carb tortillas
- 1 medium avocado, sliced
- 1/2 cup shredded cheddar cheese
- 1/4 cup chopped fresh cilantro
- Optional: hot sauce or salsa, for serving

Instructions:

1. In a small bowl, whisk together the eggs, milk, salt, and pepper until well combined.
2. Melt the butter or coconut oil in a large non-stick skillet over medium heat.
3. Add the egg mixture to the skillet and cook, stirring occasionally, until the eggs are scrambled and cooked through.
4. Warm the low-carb tortillas in the microwave or in a skillet for a few seconds on each side.
5. Divide the scrambled eggs, sliced avocado, shredded cheddar cheese, and chopped cilantro among the tortillas, placing the ingredients in the center of each tortilla.

6. Fold the sides of the tortilla inwards, then roll the tortilla tightly to form a burrito.
7. Serve the low-carb breakfast burritos with hot sauce or salsa, if desired.
8. Enjoy your delicious and healthy low-carb breakfast burrito with avocado!

CHAPTER 3

APPETIZER AND SNACK RECIPES
A. GLUTEN-FREE AND DIABETIC-FRIENDLY HUMMUS WITH VEGETABLES

Sure! Here's a recipe for gluten-free and diabetic-friendly hummus with vegetables:

Ingredients:

- 1 can (15 oz) chickpeas, drained and rinsed
- 2 cloves garlic, minced
- 1/4 cup tahini
- 1/4 cup lemon juice
- 1/4 teaspoon ground cumin
- 1/4 teaspoon paprika
- 1/4 teaspoon salt
- 2-3 tablespoons water

- Assorted vegetables for dipping (such as carrot sticks, cucumber slices, and bell pepper strips)

Instructions:

1. In a food processor or blender, combine the chickpeas, garlic, tahini, lemon juice, cumin, paprika, and salt. Pulse until the mixture is smooth and creamy, scraping down the sides of the bowl as needed.
2. With the motor running, slowly add water, 1 tablespoon at a time, until the hummus reaches your desired consistency.
3. Taste the hummus and adjust the seasoning as needed.
4. Transfer the hummus to a serving bowl and arrange the vegetables around it.
5. Serve the hummus and vegetables immediately or cover and refrigerate until ready to serve.
6. Enjoy your delicious and healthy gluten-free and diabetic-friendly hummus with vegetables!

B) SLOW-COOKED BEEF STEW WITH ROOT VEGETABLES:

Absolutely, here's a recipe for a hearty slow-cooked beef stew with root vegetables:

Ingredients:

- 2 pounds beef chuck roast, cut into 1-inch cubes
- 1/4 cup all-purpose flour
- 1 teaspoon salt
- 1/2 teaspoon black pepper
- 2 tablespoons olive oil
- 1 large onion, chopped
- 4 cloves garlic, minced
- 4 cups beef broth
- 2 tablespoons tomato paste
- 1 teaspoon dried thyme
- 1 teaspoon dried rosemary
- 1 bay leaf
- 2 large carrots, peeled and chopped
- 2 parsnips, peeled and chopped
- 2 turnips, peeled and chopped
- 1 cup chopped celery root (celeriac)
- 1 cup frozen peas

Instructions:

1. In a large mixing bowl, combine the flour, salt, and black pepper. Add the beef cubes and toss to coat evenly.
2. Heat the olive oil in a large skillet over medium-high heat. Add the beef cubes in batches and cook until browned on all sides, about 5 minutes per batch. Transfer the browned beef to a slow cooker.
3. Add the onion and garlic to the skillet and cook for 2-3 minutes until softened. Add the beef broth, tomato paste, thyme, rosemary, and bay leaf. Stir well to combine and bring the mixture to a simmer.
4. Pour the mixture over the beef in the slow cooker. Add the carrots, parsnips, turnips, and celery root. Stir to combine.
5. Cover the slow cooker and cook on low for 8-10 hours or on high for 4-6 hours, until the beef and vegetables are tender.
6. Stir in the frozen peas and cook for an additional 10-15 minutes until the peas are heated through.
7. Serve the beef stew hot, garnished with fresh herbs if desired.
8. Enjoy your delicious and comforting slow-cooked beef stew with root vegetables!

C)BAKED ZUCCHINI FRIES WITH HOMEMADE RANCH DRESSING:

Here's a recipe for baked zucchini fries with homemade ranch dressing:

Ingredients:

For the zucchini fries:

- 2 medium zucchini, cut into sticks
- 1 cup panko breadcrumbs
- 1/2 cup grated parmesan cheese
- 1/2 teaspoon garlic powder
- 1/2 teaspoon paprika
- 1/2 teaspoon salt
- 2 large eggs
- For the ranch dressing:
- 1/2 cup plain Greek yogurt

- 1/4 cup buttermilk
- 1 tablespoon chopped fresh dill
- 1 tablespoon chopped fresh chives
- 1 teaspoon garlic powder
- 1 teaspoon onion powder
- 1/2 teaspoon salt
- 1/4 teaspoon black pepper

Instructions:

1. Preheat your oven to 425°F (220°C).
2. Line a baking sheet with parchment paper and set aside.
3. In a shallow dish, combine the panko breadcrumbs, parmesan cheese, garlic powder, paprika, and salt.
4. In another shallow dish, beat the eggs.
5. Dip each zucchini stick into the egg mixture, then into the breadcrumb mixture, pressing to coat well.
6. Place the coated zucchini sticks on the prepared baking sheet, leaving space between each stick.
7. Bake for 20-25 minutes or until the zucchini is tender and the coating is golden brown and crispy.

8. While the zucchini fries are baking, prepare the ranch dressing. In a small mixing bowl, whisk together the Greek yogurt, buttermilk, dill, chives, garlic powder, onion powder, salt, and black pepper.
9. Serve the zucchini fries hot, accompanied by the homemade ranch dressing for dipping.
10. Enjoy your delicious and healthy baked zucchini fries with homemade ranch dressing!

D)GLUTEN-FREE BAKED TORTILLA CHIPS WITH SALSA:

Here's a recipe for gluten-free baked tortilla chips with salsa:

Ingredients for Tortilla Chips:

- 6-8 gluten-free tortillas
- 2 tablespoons olive oil
- Salt, to taste
- Ingredients for Salsa:
- 4 medium tomatoes, diced
- 1 small onion, finely chopped
- 2 cloves garlic, minced
- 1 jalapeño pepper, seeded and finely chopped (optional)

- 1/4 cup chopped fresh cilantro
- Juice of 1 lime
- Salt and pepper, to taste

Instructions for Tortilla Chips:

- Preheat the oven to 350°F (180°C).
- Stack the tortillas and cut them into 8 wedges.
- Arrange the tortilla wedges on a large baking sheet in a single layer.
- Drizzle the olive oil over the tortilla wedges, then sprinkle salt on top.
- Bake the tortilla chips for 10-12 minutes, or until they are golden brown and crispy.
- Remove the tortilla chips from the oven and let them cool for a few minutes.

Instructions for Salsa:

- In a medium mixing bowl, combine the diced tomatoes, chopped onion, minced garlic, chopped jalapeño (if using), chopped cilantro, and lime juice.
- Stir well to combine, then season with salt and pepper to taste.
- Serve the salsa in a small bowl alongside the baked tortilla chips.

- Enjoy your delicious gluten-free baked tortilla chips with salsa!

E) ROASTED CHICKPEAS WITH HERBS AND SPICES

Here's a recipe for roasted chickpeas with herbs and spices:

Ingredients:

- 2 cans chickpeas, drained and rinsed
- 2 tablespoons olive oil
- 1 teaspoon paprika
- 1/2 teaspoon cumin
- 1/2 teaspoon garlic powder
- 1/2 teaspoon onion powder
- 1/2 teaspoon dried oregano
- 1/2 teaspoon dried thyme
- 1/2 teaspoon salt
- Freshly ground black pepper, to taste

Instructions:

1. Preheat the oven to 400°F (200°C).
2. Spread the chickpeas out on a baking sheet lined with parchment paper or a silicone mat.

3. Drizzle the olive oil over the chickpeas, then sprinkle the paprika, cumin, garlic powder, onion powder, oregano, thyme, salt, and black pepper over the top.
4. Use your hands to toss the chickpeas until they are evenly coated with the oil and spices.
5. Roast the chickpeas in the preheated oven for 25-30 minutes, or until they are crispy and lightly browned.
6. Remove the chickpeas from the oven and let them cool for a few minutes before serving.
7. Enjoy your delicious and healthy roasted chickpeas with herbs and spices as a snack or side dish!

F) CHEESE CUCUMBER BITES

Ingredients:

- 1 large cucumber
- 4 oz cream cheese, softened
- 1/4 cup shredded cheddar cheese
- 2 tablespoons finely chopped fresh chives
- Salt and pepper, to taste

Instructions:

1. Cut the cucumber into 1-inch thick rounds. Use a small spoon or melon baller to scoop out the center of each round, creating a small well for the filling.
2. In a medium bowl, mix together the cream cheese, shredded cheddar cheese, and chopped chives until well combined.
3. Season the cheese mixture with salt and pepper to taste.
4. Spoon the cheese mixture into the wells of the cucumber rounds, filling each one to the top.
5. Arrange the filled cucumber rounds on a serving platter and chill until ready to serve.
6. Optional: Garnish with additional chopped chives or other herbs, if desired.
7. Serve and enjoy these tasty and refreshing Cheese Cucumber Bites!

H) SWEET POTATO AND KALE FRITTERS:

Sure, here's a recipe for Sweet Potato and Kale Fritters:

Ingredients:

- 2 medium sweet potatoes, peeled and grated
- 2 cups kale, finely chopped
- 1/2 cup all-purpose flour
- 1/4 cup cornstarch
- 1/4 cup grated Parmesan cheese
- 2 cloves garlic, minced
- 1 teaspoon smoked paprika
- 1 teaspoon salt
- 1/4 teaspoon black pepper
- 2 large eggs, beaten

- 1/4 cup olive oil, for frying

Instructions:

1. In a large mixing bowl, combine the grated sweet potatoes and chopped kale.
2. In a separate bowl, whisk together the flour, cornstarch, Parmesan cheese, minced garlic, smoked paprika, salt, and black pepper.
3. Pour the dry mixture into the bowl with the sweet potato and kale. Stir well to combine.
4. Add the beaten eggs to the mixture and stir until everything is well coated.
5. Heat the olive oil in a large skillet over medium heat.
6. Scoop a heaping tablespoon of the mixture and drop it into the hot oil, flattening it slightly with the back of the spoon. Repeat until the skillet is full, but be careful not to overcrowd the pan.
7. Cook for 2-3 minutes on each side, or until golden brown and crispy. Remove from the skillet and place on a paper towel-lined plate to drain any excess oil.
8. Repeat with the remaining mixture, adding more oil to the skillet as needed.

9. Serve warm and enjoy your Sweet Potato and Kale Fritters!

CHAPTER 4

MAIN DISH RECIPES:

A. GRILLED CHICKEN WITH LEMON AND HERBS:

Here's a recipe for grilled chicken with lemon and herbs:

Ingredients:

- 4 boneless, skinless chicken breasts
- 2 lemons, juiced and zested
- 1/4 cup olive oil
- 2 cloves garlic, minced
- 1 teaspoon dried oregano
- 1 teaspoon dried thyme

- 1 teaspoon salt
- 1/2 teaspoon black pepper

Instructions:

1. In a mixing bowl, whisk together the lemon juice, lemon zest, olive oil, garlic, oregano, thyme, salt, and black pepper to make the marinade.
2. Add the chicken breasts to the marinade and toss to coat evenly. Cover the bowl with plastic wrap and refrigerate for at least 30 minutes or up to 2 hours.
3. Preheat your grill to medium-high heat.
4. Remove the chicken breasts from the marinade and discard the remaining marinade.
5. Place the chicken breasts on the grill and cook for 6-8 minutes per side or until the internal temperature reaches 165°F (75°C).
6. Remove the chicken from the grill and let it rest for 5 minutes before slicing.
7. Serve the grilled chicken hot, garnished with fresh herbs or lemon wedges if desired.
8. Enjoy your delicious and flavorful grilled chicken with lemon and herbs!

B) SLOW-COOKED BEEF STEW WITH ROOT VEGETABLES:

Ingredients:

- 2 lbs (900g) beef chuck, cut into 1-inch cubes
- 2 tablespoons olive oil
- 1 onion, chopped
- 3 cloves garlic, minced
- 2 cups beef broth
- 1 cup red wine
- 2 bay leaves
- 1 teaspoon dried thyme
- 1 teaspoon salt
- 1/2 teaspoon black pepper
- 4 carrots, peeled and cut into chunks
- 4 parsnips, peeled and cut into chunks
- 2 potatoes, peeled and cut into chunks

Instructions:

1. In a large skillet over medium-high heat, heat the olive oil. Add the beef and cook until browned on all sides, about 5-7 minutes.
2. Transfer the beef to a slow cooker.

3. Add the onion and garlic to the skillet and cook for 2-3 minutes, or until softened.
4. Add the beef broth and red wine to the skillet, scraping any browned bits from the bottom of the pan.
5. Pour the liquid mixture into the slow cooker with the beef.
6. Add the bay leaves, thyme, salt, and black pepper to the slow cooker and stir to combine.
7. Add the carrots, parsnips, and potatoes to the slow cooker and stir to combine.
8. Cover the slow cooker and cook on low heat for 6-8 hours or until the beef and vegetables are tender.
9. Serve the beef stew hot, garnished with fresh herbs if desired.
10. Enjoy your delicious and hearty slow-cooked beef stew with root vegetables!

C)SHRIMP STIR-FRY WITH BROWN RICE AND VEGETABLES

Here's a recipe for shrimp stir-fry with brown rice and vegetables:

Ingredients:

- 1 lb (450g) large shrimp, peeled and deveined
- 2 cups cooked brown rice
- 2 tablespoons vegetable oil
- 1 onion, chopped
- 3 cloves garlic, minced
- 1 red bell pepper, sliced
- 1 green bell pepper, sliced
- 1 cup sliced mushrooms
- 1 cup snow peas, trimmed

- 2 tablespoons soy sauce
- 1 tablespoon honey
- 1 tablespoon cornstarch
- 1/2 teaspoon salt
- 1/4 teaspoon black pepper

Instructions:

1. In a small mixing bowl, whisk together the soy sauce, honey, cornstarch, salt, and black pepper to make the sauce. Set aside.
2. Heat the vegetable oil in a large wok or skillet over high heat.
3. Add the onion and garlic to the wok and cook for 2-3 minutes, or until softened.
4. Add the red and green bell peppers, mushrooms, and snow peas to the wok and stir-fry for 3-4 minutes, or until the vegetables are tender-crisp.
5. Add the shrimp to the wok and stir-fry for 2-3 minutes, or until the shrimp are pink and cooked through.
6. Pour the sauce into the wok and stir-fry for another 1-2 minutes, or until the sauce has thickened and coated the shrimp and vegetables.

7. Serve the shrimp stir-fry over the cooked brown rice.
8. Enjoy your delicious and healthy shrimp stir-fry with brown rice and vegetables!

D) GLUTEN-FREE QUINOA AND BLACK BEAN SALAD WITH AVOCADO DRESSING

Here's a recipe for Gluten-Free Quinoa and Black Bean Salad with Avocado Dressing:

Ingredients:

- 1 cup quinoa
- 1 can black beans, drained and rinsed
- 1 red bell pepper, diced
- 1/2 red onion, diced
- 1/4 cup chopped fresh cilantro
- 1 avocado, diced
- Juice of 1 lime
- Salt and pepper, to taste

For the Avocado Dressing:

- 1 avocado, pitted and peeled
- 1/4 cup plain Greek yogurt
- Juice of 1 lime
- 1 clove garlic, minced

- 1/4 teaspoon salt
- 1/4 teaspoon black pepper
- 2 tablespoons water (more or less, as needed to reach desired consistency)

Instructions:

1. Rinse quinoa in a fine mesh strainer and add it to a medium saucepan with 2 cups of water. Bring to a boil, reduce heat to low, cover, and simmer for 15-20 minutes or until water is absorbed and quinoa is tender. Fluff with a fork and let cool.
2. In a large mixing bowl, combine the cooked quinoa, black beans, diced bell pepper, diced red onion, and chopped cilantro.
3. In a blender or food processor, combine the avocado, Greek yogurt, lime juice, minced garlic, salt, black pepper, and water. Blend until smooth and creamy.
4. Pour the avocado dressing over the quinoa and black bean mixture and toss to combine.
5. Add the diced avocado and lime juice to the salad and toss gently.
6. Taste and adjust seasoning with salt and pepper as needed.

7. Serve the Gluten-Free Quinoa and Black Bean Salad with Avocado Dressing chilled or at room temperature. Enjoy!

E) SPICY SHRIMP AND VEGETABLE STIR-FRY WITH BROWN RICE

Here's a recipe for Spicy Shrimp and Vegetable Stir-Fry with Brown Rice:

Ingredients:

- 1 pound shrimp, peeled and deveined
- 2 tablespoons olive oil
- 2 cloves garlic, minced
- 1 teaspoon grated fresh ginger
- 1 red bell pepper, sliced

- 1 green bell pepper, sliced
- 1 onion, sliced
- 2 cups broccoli florets
- 1/2 teaspoon red pepper flakes
- 1/4 cup soy sauce
- 2 tablespoons honey
- 1 tablespoon cornstarch
- 1 tablespoon water
- 4 cups cooked brown rice

Instructions:

1. Heat the olive oil in a large skillet or wok over high heat.
2. Add the minced garlic and grated ginger to the skillet and cook for 1-2 minutes until fragrant.
3. Add the sliced red and green bell peppers and sliced onion to the skillet and cook for 2-3 minutes until softened.
4. Add the broccoli florets to the skillet and cook for an additional 2-3 minutes until they begin to soften.
5. Add the shrimp and red pepper flakes to the skillet and cook for 3-4 minutes until the shrimp are pink and cooked through.

6. In a small bowl, whisk together the soy sauce, honey, cornstarch, and water until smooth.
7. Pour the soy sauce mixture over the shrimp and vegetables in the skillet and stir to coat everything evenly.
8. Cook for an additional 1-2 minutes until the sauce thickens and the shrimp and vegetables are coated.
9. Serve the Spicy Shrimp and Vegetable Stir-Fry over a bed of cooked brown rice. Enjoy!

G) BAKED CHICKEN THIGHS WITH LEMON AND HERBS:

Here's a recipe for Baked Chicken Thighs with Lemon and Herbs:

Ingredients:

- 8 bone-in, skin-on chicken thighs
- 2 tablespoons olive oil
- 2 cloves garlic, minced
- 1 tablespoon chopped fresh thyme
- 1 tablespoon chopped fresh rosemary
- 1 lemon, juiced and zested
- Salt and pepper, to taste

Instructions:

1. Preheat the oven to 425°F (218°C).
2. In a small mixing bowl, combine the olive oil, minced garlic, chopped thyme, chopped rosemary, lemon juice, and lemon zest. Stir well to combine.
3. Place the chicken thighs in a large baking dish or cast-iron skillet. Season the chicken generously with salt and pepper on both sides.
4. Pour the lemon and herb mixture over the chicken, making sure to coat each piece evenly.
5. Bake the chicken in the preheated oven for 35-40 minutes, or until the skin is golden brown and crispy and the chicken is cooked through with an internal temperature of 165°F (74°C).
6. Remove the chicken from the oven and let it rest for 5 minutes before serving.
7. Serve the Baked Chicken Thighs with Lemon and Herbs with your favorite sides, such as roasted vegetables, potatoes, or a salad. Enjoy!

CHAPTER 4

SIDE DISH RECIPES:
A. ROASTED BRUSSELS SPROUTS WITH GARLIC AND PARMESAN

Here's a recipe for roasted Brussels sprouts with garlic and Parmesan:

Ingredients:

- 1 lb (450g) Brussels sprouts, trimmed and halved
- 2 tablespoons olive oil
- 4 cloves garlic, minced
- 1/4 teaspoon salt
- 1/4 teaspoon black pepper
- 1/4 cup grated Parmesan cheese

Instructions:

1. Preheat your oven to 400°F (200°C).
2. In a mixing bowl, toss the Brussels sprouts with the olive oil, minced garlic, salt, and black pepper to coat evenly.
3. Spread the Brussels sprouts out in a single layer on a baking sheet.

4. Roast the Brussels sprouts in the oven for 20-25 minutes, or until they are tender and caramelized.
5. Remove the Brussels sprouts from the oven and sprinkle the grated Parmesan cheese over the top.
6. Return the baking sheet to the oven and continue roasting for another 2-3 minutes, or until the cheese is melted and bubbly.
7. Serve the roasted Brussels sprouts hot, garnished with additional Parmesan cheese and chopped herbs if desired.
8. Enjoy your delicious and flavorful roasted Brussels sprouts with garlic and Parmesan!

B) QUINOA PILAF WITH ROASTED VEGETABLES AND CHICKPEAS

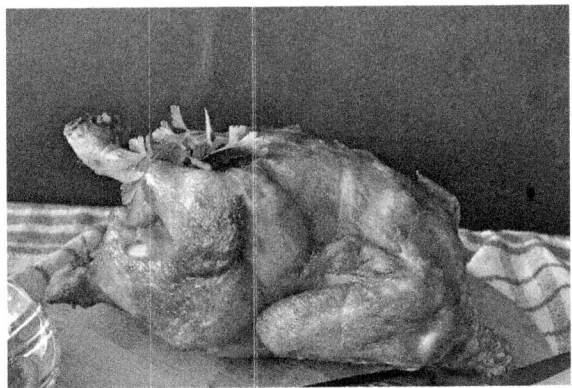

Here's a recipe for quinoa pilaf with roasted vegetables and chickpeas:

Ingredients:

- 1 cup quinoa, rinsed
- 2 cups water or vegetable broth
- 1 small sweet potato, peeled and cut into cubes
- 1 small red bell pepper, seeded and diced
- 1 small zucchini, diced
- 1 cup canned chickpeas, drained and rinsed
- 2 tablespoons olive oil
- 2 teaspoons ground cumin
- 1/2 teaspoon salt
- 1/4 teaspoon black pepper
- 1/4 cup chopped fresh parsley
- 1/4 cup crumbled feta cheese

Instructions:

1. Preheat your oven to 400°F (200°C).
2. In a medium saucepan, combine the quinoa and water or vegetable broth. Bring to a boil over high heat, then reduce the heat to low and simmer for 15-20 minutes, or until the quinoa is cooked through and the liquid has been absorbed.

3. In a large mixing bowl, toss the sweet potato, red bell pepper, zucchini, and chickpeas with the olive oil, ground cumin, salt, and black pepper to coat evenly.
4. Spread the vegetable mixture out in a single layer on a baking sheet.
5. Roast the vegetables in the oven for 20-25 minutes, or until they are tender and caramelized.
6. In a large mixing bowl, combine the cooked quinoa and roasted vegetables. Toss to combine.
7. Serve the quinoa pilaf hot, garnished with chopped fresh parsley and crumbled feta cheese.
8. Enjoy your delicious and healthy quinoa pilaf with roasted vegetables and chickpeas!

C. STEAMED BROCCOLI WITH LEMON AND ALMONDS

Here's a recipe for steamed broccoli with lemon and almonds:

Ingredients:

- 1 lb (450g) broccoli florets
- 1/4 cup sliced almonds
- 2 tablespoons unsalted butter
- 1 tablespoon lemon juice
- 1 teaspoon lemon zest
- 1/4 teaspoon salt
- 1/4 teaspoon black pepper

Instructions:

1. Bring a pot of water to a boil over high heat. Add the broccoli florets and blanch them for 2-3 minutes, or until they are bright green and slightly tender.
2. Drain the broccoli florets in a colander and set them aside.
3. In a small skillet, toast the sliced almonds over medium heat until they are golden brown and fragrant.
4. In a small saucepan, melt the butter over low heat.

5. Remove the saucepan from the heat and stir in the lemon juice, lemon zest, salt, and black pepper.
6. Place the steamed broccoli florets in a serving dish and pour the lemon butter sauce over the top.
7. Sprinkle the toasted almonds over the broccoli florets.
8. Serve the steamed broccoli hot, garnished with additional lemon zest and sliced almonds if desired.
9. Enjoy your delicious and nutritious steamed broccoli with lemon and almonds!

G) ROASTED BRUSSELS SPROUTS WITH GARLIC AND PARMESAN:

Certainly, here's a recipe for Roasted Brussels Sprouts with Garlic and Parmesan:

Ingredients:

- 1 pound Brussels sprouts
- 3 cloves garlic, minced
- 2 tablespoons olive oil
- 1/2 teaspoon salt
- 1/4 teaspoon black pepper
- 1/4 cup grated Parmesan cheese

Instructions:

- Preheat your oven to 400°F (200°C).
- Rinse and trim the Brussels sprouts, removing any damaged outer leaves.
- Cut the Brussels sprouts in half, lengthwise.
- In a large mixing bowl, combine the halved Brussels sprouts with minced garlic, olive oil, salt, and black pepper. Toss to coat the Brussels sprouts evenly.
- Spread the Brussels sprouts evenly on a baking sheet, cut side down.
- Roast the Brussels sprouts in the oven for 20-25 minutes, or until they are tender and golden brown. Flip them halfway through the cooking time to ensure even browning.
- Remove the Brussels sprouts from the oven and sprinkle the grated Parmesan cheese over the top.
- Return the Brussels sprouts to the oven for another 5-7 minutes or until the cheese is melted and slightly browned.
- Remove the baking sheet from the oven and let the Brussels sprouts cool for a few minutes before serving.

- Serve hot and enjoy your Roasted Brussels Sprouts with Garlic and Parmesan!

H) GRILLED ASPARAGUS WITH LEMON AND OLIVE OIL:

Sure, here's a recipe for Grilled Asparagus with Lemon and Olive Oil:

Ingredients:

- 1 pound asparagus spears
- 2 tablespoons olive oil
- 1 tablespoon lemon juice
- 1/2 teaspoon salt
- 1/4 teaspoon black pepper

Instructions:

- Preheat your grill to medium-high heat.

- Rinse the asparagus and snap off the woody ends.
- In a mixing bowl, combine the olive oil, lemon juice, salt, and black pepper.
- Add the asparagus to the bowl and toss to coat evenly.
- Place the asparagus spears on the grill, perpendicular to the grates, to prevent them from falling through.
- Grill the asparagus for 5-7 minutes, or until they are tender and slightly charred, turning them occasionally.
- Remove the asparagus from the grill and transfer them to a serving platter.
- Drizzle any remaining lemon and olive oil mixture over the grilled asparagus.
- Serve hot and enjoy your Grilled Asparagus with Lemon and Olive Oil!

I)CREAMY MASHED CAULIFLOWER WITH GARLIC AND HERBS:

Sure, here's a recipe for creamy mashed cauliflower with garlic and herbs:

Ingredients:

- 1 head of cauliflower, chopped into small pieces
- 2 cloves of garlic, minced
- 2 tbsp butter
- 2 tbsp cream cheese
- 1/4 cup milk
- 1 tbsp fresh parsley, chopped
- 1 tbsp fresh chives, chopped
- Salt and pepper, to taste

Instructions:

1. Steam the chopped cauliflower until it's tender. You can do this by placing it in a steamer basket over boiling water, or by microwaving it in a covered bowl with a few tablespoons of water for 5-7 minutes.
2. While the cauliflower is steaming, melt the butter in a small saucepan over medium heat. Add the minced garlic and sauté for 1-2 minutes, until fragrant.
3. Add the cream cheese to the pan and stir until it's melted and combined with the butter and garlic.
4. Once the cauliflower is tender, transfer it to a large mixing bowl. Add the cream cheese

mixture, milk, parsley, chives, salt, and pepper.
5. Use an immersion blender, or a regular blender or food processor, to blend the ingredients together until the mixture is smooth and creamy.
6. Taste and adjust the seasoning as needed.
7. Serve the mashed cauliflower warm, garnished with additional chopped herbs if desired. Enjoy!

J) STEAMED BROCCOLI WITH LEMON AND ALMONDS:

Certainly, here is a recipe for steamed broccoli with lemon and almonds:

Ingredients:

- 1 pound broccoli florets
- 1/4 cup slivered almonds
- 2 tablespoons olive oil
- 2 tablespoons lemon juice
- 1 teaspoon grated lemon zest
- Salt and pepper to taste

Instructions:

- Bring a large pot of water to a boil. Add the broccoli florets and steam for 3-5 minutes, or until the broccoli is tender-crisp.
- While the broccoli is steaming, heat a small skillet over medium heat. Add the slivered almonds and toast, stirring frequently, until they are lightly browned and fragrant. Remove from heat and set aside.
- In a small bowl, whisk together the olive oil, lemon juice, and grated lemon zest.
- Once the broccoli is steamed, transfer it to a serving dish. Drizzle the lemon and olive oil mixture over the top of the broccoli.
- Sprinkle the toasted almonds over the top of the broccoli.
- Season the broccoli with salt and pepper to taste.

- Serve the steamed broccoli warm, garnished with additional lemon zest and/or chopped herbs if desired. Enjoy!

CHAPTER 5

DESSERT RECIPES

A. FLOURLESS CHOCOLATE CAKE WITH FRESH BERRIES

Here's a recipe for flourless chocolate cake with fresh berries

Ingredients:

- 10 oz (280g) dark chocolate, chopped
- 1 cup (2 sticks) unsalted butter, cut into small pieces
- 1 cup granulated sugar
- 6 large eggs, room temperature
- 1/2 cup unsweetened cocoa powder

- 1/4 teaspoon salt
- Fresh berries, for serving

Instructions:

1. Preheat your oven to 350°F (175°C).
2. In a heatproof mixing bowl, melt the chopped dark chocolate and butter over a double boiler or in the microwave, stirring occasionally, until they are smooth and fully melted.
3. Remove the mixing bowl from the heat and whisk in the granulated sugar until the mixture is smooth.
4. Whisk in the eggs, one at a time, until fully incorporated.
5. Sift the cocoa powder and salt into the mixing bowl and whisk until the batter is smooth.
6. Pour the batter into a greased 9-inch (23cm) springform pan and smooth the top with a spatula.
7. Bake the flourless chocolate cake in the preheated oven for 35-40 minutes, or until a toothpick inserted into the center comes out clean.

8. Let the cake cool in the pan for 10 minutes before removing it from the pan and transferring it to a wire rack to cool completely.
9. Serve the flourless chocolate cake with fresh berries on top.
10. Enjoy your decadent and gluten-free flourless chocolate cake with fresh berries!

B) GLUTEN-FREE AND DIABETIC-FRIENDLY APPLE CRISP

Here's a recipe for gluten-free and diabetic-friendly apple crisp:

Ingredients:

- 6 medium apples, peeled, cored, and thinly sliced
- 1/2 cup almond flour

- 1/2 cup gluten-free rolled oats
- 1/4 cup chopped pecans
- 1/4 cup unsalted butter, melted
- 2 tablespoons pure maple syrup
- 1 teaspoon ground cinnamon
- 1/4 teaspoon ground nutmeg
- 1/4 teaspoon salt

Instructions:

1. Preheat your oven to 350°F (175°C).
2. Arrange the sliced apples in a 9x9-inch (23x23cm) baking dish.
3. In a mixing bowl, combine the almond flour, gluten-free rolled oats, chopped pecans, melted unsalted butter, pure maple syrup, ground cinnamon, ground nutmeg, and salt.
4. Mix well with a fork or a pastry cutter until the mixture is crumbly and well combined.
5. Sprinkle the crumble mixture over the top of the sliced apples in the baking dish.
6. Bake the apple crisp in the preheated oven for 35-40 minutes, or until the top is golden brown and the apples are tender.
7. Let the apple crisp cool for 5-10 minutes before serving.

8. Serve the gluten-free and diabetic-friendly apple crisp warm, topped with a dollop of whipped cream or a scoop of vanilla ice cream if desired.
9. Enjoy your delicious and healthy gluten-free and diabetic-friendly apple crisp!

C) COCONUT MILK PUDDING WITH MANGO AND TOASTED COCONUT

Here's a recipe for coconut milk pudding with mango and toasted coconut:

Ingredients:

- 2 cups coconut milk
- 1/2 cup sugar

- 1/4 cup cornstarch
- 1/4 teaspoon salt
- 1 teaspoon vanilla extract
- 1 ripe mango, peeled and chopped
- 1/4 cup shredded unsweetened coconut, toasted

Instructions:

1. In a medium saucepan, whisk together the coconut milk, sugar, cornstarch, and salt until well combined.
2. Place the saucepan over medium heat and cook, whisking constantly, until the mixture comes to a boil and thickens, about 5-7 minutes.
3. Remove the saucepan from the heat and whisk in the vanilla extract.
4. Pour the coconut milk pudding into a large bowl and cover the surface with plastic wrap to prevent a skin from forming.
5. Chill the pudding in the refrigerator for at least 2 hours, or until it is set and firm.
6. Once the pudding is chilled and set, spoon it into individual serving bowls or glasses.
7. Top each serving with chopped mango and toasted shredded coconut.

8. Serve the coconut milk pudding with mango and toasted coconut chilled.
9. Enjoy your delicious and refreshing coconut milk pudding with mango and toasted coconut!

D) SMOKED SALMON AND CREAM

Ingredients:

- 8 oz smoked salmon
- 4 oz cream cheese
- 1/4 cup heavy cream
- 1 tablespoon fresh dill, chopped
- Salt and pepper, to taste
- Lemon wedges, for serving
- Crackers or sliced bread, for serving

Instructions:

- In a medium bowl, mix together the cream cheese, heavy cream, and fresh dill until well combined.
- Flake the smoked salmon into small pieces and add to the cream cheese mixture. Gently stir to combine.
- Taste and season with salt and pepper, as desired.

- Transfer the smoked salmon and cream mixture to a serving dish and garnish with additional fresh dill, if desired.
- Serve with lemon wedges and crackers or sliced bread. Enjoy!

E) ONE-POT MEXICAN CAULIFLOWER RICE WITH BEEF:

Sure, here's a recipe for One-Pot Mexican Cauliflower Rice with Beef:

Ingredients:

- 1 pound ground beef
- 1 medium-sized head of cauliflower
- 1 red bell pepper, diced
- 1 yellow onion, diced
- 2 cloves garlic, minced
- 1 tablespoon chili powder
- 1 teaspoon cumin
- 1 teaspoon paprika
- 1/2 teaspoon salt
- 1/4 teaspoon black pepper
- 1 can (14.5 ounces) diced tomatoes
- 1 cup beef broth
- 1 cup frozen corn
- 1/4 cup chopped fresh cilantro

- Juice of 1 lime

Instructions:

1. Begin by washing and preparing the cauliflower. Cut it into small florets and pulse in a food processor until it resembles rice.
2. Heat a large skillet over medium-high heat. Add the ground beef and cook until browned, breaking it up with a spoon as it cooks.
3. Add the diced bell pepper, onion, and garlic to the skillet. Cook for 2-3 minutes until the vegetables have softened.
4. Stir in the chili powder, cumin, paprika, salt, and black pepper. Mix until the spices are evenly distributed.
5. Add the diced tomatoes, beef broth, and frozen corn to the skillet. Bring to a boil and then reduce the heat to low.
6. Add the cauliflower rice to the skillet and stir to combine. Cover and simmer for 10-15 minutes, stirring occasionally, until the cauliflower is tender and the liquid has been absorbed.

7. Remove the skillet from the heat and stir in the chopped cilantro and lime juice.
8. Serve hot and enjoy your One-Pot Mexican Cauliflower Rice with Beef!

F) ALMOND FLOUR SHORTBREAD COOKIES:

Here's a recipe for almond flour shortbread cookies:

Ingredients:

- 1 cup almond flour
- 1/4 cup coconut flour
- 1/4 cup granulated sugar
- 1/4 teaspoon salt
- 1/2 cup unsalted butter, softened
- 1 teaspoon vanilla extract

Instructions:

1. Preheat your oven to 350°F (175°C). Line a baking sheet with parchment paper.
2. In a medium mixing bowl, whisk together the almond flour, coconut flour, sugar, and salt.
3. Add the softened butter and vanilla extract to the dry ingredients, and use a fork or pastry cutter to blend the mixture together until it forms a cohesive dough.
4. Use your hands to roll the dough into small balls, about 1 inch in diameter.
5. Place the dough balls on the prepared baking sheet, leaving about 1 inch of space between each cookie.
6. Use a fork to press down lightly on each cookie, flattening it slightly.
7. Bake for 12-15 minutes, or until the edges of the cookies are golden brown.
8. Allow the cookies to cool on the baking sheet for 5 minutes before transferring them to a wire rack to cool completely.
9. Serve and enjoy your almond flour shortbread cookies! These cookies can be stored in an airtight container at room temperature for up to 5 days.

G) LOW-SUGAR FRUIT AND YOGURT PARFAIT

Here is a recipe for a low-sugar fruit and yogurt parfait:

Ingredients:

- 1 cup plain Greek yogurt
- 1 teaspoon honey
- 1/2 teaspoon vanilla extract
- 1 cup mixed fresh fruit (such as berries, sliced peaches, or chopped mango)
- 1/4 cup granola or chopped nuts

Instructions:

1. In a small bowl, mix together the Greek yogurt, honey, and vanilla extract until well combined.
2. Spoon a small amount of the yogurt mixture into the bottom of a serving glass or jar.
3. Add a layer of mixed fresh fruit on top of the yogurt.
4. Add another layer of the yogurt mixture on top of the fruit.
5. Sprinkle a layer of granola or chopped nuts over the yogurt.
6. Repeat layers until you reach the top of the glass or jar, ending with a layer of fruit on top.
7. Serve and enjoy your low-sugar fruit and yogurt parfait! You can store any leftover parfait in an airtight container in the refrigerator for up to 2 days.

CONCLUSION:

Tips for Successful Gluten-FreeHere are some tips for successful gluten-free living:

1. Educate yourself: Learn about gluten and the foods that contain it. Familiarize yourself with gluten-free alternatives to your favorite foods.
2. Read labels carefully: Look for gluten-free labeling or certifications on products. Check ingredients lists for hidden sources of gluten such as malt, barley, and wheat.
3. Plan ahead: When eating out, research gluten-free options ahead of time or bring your own gluten-free snacks or meals.
4. Cook at home: Cooking your own meals allows you to control the ingredients and ensure that they are gluten-free.
5. Find gluten-free substitutes: There are many gluten-free substitutes available for flour, pasta, and bread. Experiment with different brands and find ones that work for you.
6. Don't assume all "gluten-free" products are healthy: Gluten-free products can still be

high in sugar, fat, and calories. Be sure to read the nutrition labels.
7. Be patient: It may take some time to adjust to a gluten-free diet, but with patience and persistence, it will become easier and more natural.
8. Seek support: Join a support group or find a community of others who are also living gluten-free. They can offer advice, recipes, and emotional support.

FINAL THOUGHTS AND RECOMMENDATIONS:

In conclusion, adopting a gluten-free diet can be a challenge, but it is also necessary for those with gluten sensitivities or celiac disease. It is important to educate yourself on the foods and ingredients that contain gluten, read labels carefully, plan ahead, and find gluten-free substitutes. Additionally, it's essential to maintain a balanced and nutritious diet, as gluten-free products can still be high in sugar and fat.

If you are struggling to adjust to a gluten-free diet, don't hesitate to seek support from a healthcare professional, a registered dietitian, or a support group. They can provide guidance, information, and emotional support.

Finally, it's worth noting that a gluten-free diet is not necessarily a healthier diet for people without gluten sensitivities or celiac disease. It's always best to consult with a healthcare professional or a registered dietitian before making any significant changes to your diet.

Overall, by being mindful and informed about your dietary needs and choices, you can successfully manage a gluten-free lifestyle and maintain good health.

CHAPTER 6

30 DAYS MEAL PLAN

Sure, here's a sample 30-day meal plan for a gluten-free diabetic cookbook:

DAY 1:

Breakfast: Gluten-free oatmeal with sliced banana and almond milk

Snack: Apple slices with almond butter

Lunch: Grilled chicken salad with mixed greens, cherry tomatoes, cucumber, and balsamic vinaigrette

Snack: Carrot sticks with hummus

Dinner: Baked salmon with roasted Brussels sprouts and quinoa

DAY 2:

Breakfast: Scrambled eggs with sautéed spinach and mushrooms

Snack: Plain Greek yogurt with sliced strawberries

Lunch: Turkey wrap with gluten-free tortilla, avocado, lettuce, and tomato

Snack: Roasted almonds

Dinner: Slow cooker beef stew with carrots, celery, and sweet potatoes

DAY 3:

Breakfast: Smoothie with spinach, banana, almond milk, and chia seeds

Snack: Rice cakes with peanut butter and sliced banana

Lunch: Tuna salad with mixed greens, cucumber, and cherry tomatoes

Snack: Celery sticks with cream cheese

Dinner: Grilled shrimp with zucchini noodles and tomato sauce

DAY 4:

Breakfast: Gluten-free pancakes with blueberries and maple syrup

Snack: Orange slices

Lunch: Chicken salad with mixed greens, avocado, and cherry tomatoes

Snack: Baby carrots with ranch dressing

Dinner: Stuffed bell peppers with ground turkey, brown rice, and tomato sauce

DAY 5:

Breakfast: Veggie omelet with spinach, mushrooms, and red bell pepper

Snack: Rice cakes with almond butter and banana slices

Lunch: Tuna salad lettuce wraps with cucumber and tomato

Snack: Grapes

Dinner: Gluten-free spaghetti with turkey meatballs and marinara sauce

DAY 6:

Breakfast: Gluten-free waffles with sliced strawberries and whipped cream

Snack: Hard-boiled egg

Lunch: Grilled chicken Caesar salad with gluten-free croutons

Snack: Roasted pumpkin seeds

Dinner: Baked chicken with roasted sweet potato and green beans

DAY 7:

Breakfast: Smoothie with almond milk, banana, spinach, and peanut butter

Snack: Apple slices with almond butter

Lunch: Turkey and avocado sandwich on gluten-free bread with mixed greens and tomato

Snack: Sugar snap peas with hummus

Dinner: Grilled steak with roasted Brussels sprouts and sweet potato

DAY 8:

Breakfast: Gluten-free oatmeal with sliced apple and cinnamon

Snack: Carrot sticks with ranch dressing

Lunch: Greek salad with mixed greens, cucumber, tomato, and feta cheese

Snack: Trail mix

DINNER: Slow cooker beef chili with gluten-free cornbread

DAY 9:

Breakfast: Scrambled eggs with diced bell pepper and gluten-free toast

Snack: Plain Greek yogurt with blueberries and honey

Lunch: Grilled chicken salad with mixed greens, cherry tomatoes, and cucumber

Snack: Roasted almonds

Dinner: Baked salmon with quinoa and roasted asparagus

DAY 10:

Breakfast: Smoothie with almond milk, banana, spinach, and chia seeds

Snack: Rice cakes with peanut butter and sliced banana

Lunch: Turkey and avocado lettuce wraps with cucumber and tomato

Snack: Baby carrots with hummus

Dinner: Stuffed bell peppers with ground turkey, brown rice, and tomato sauce

DAY 11:

Breakfast: Gluten-free pancakes with sliced strawberries and whipped cream

Snack: Hard-boiled egg

Lunch: Chicken Caesar

DAY 12:

Breakfast: Scrambled eggs with sautéed spinach and mushrooms

Snack: Plain Greek yogurt with sliced strawberries

Lunch: Grilled chicken salad with mixed greens, cherry tomatoes, cucumber, and balsamic vinaigrette

Snack: Carrot sticks with hummus

Dinner: Slow cooker beef stew with carrots, celery, and sweet potatoes

DAY 13:

Breakfast: Smoothie with spinach, banana, almond milk, and chia seeds

Snack: Rice cakes with almond butter and banana slices

Lunch: Tuna salad with mixed greens, avocado, and cherry tomatoes

Snack: Celery sticks with cream cheese

Dinner: Grilled shrimp with zucchini noodles and tomato sauce

DAY 14:
Breakfast: Gluten-free oatmeal with sliced banana and almond milk

Snack: Apple slices with almond butter

Lunch: Turkey wrap with gluten-free tortilla, avocado, lettuce, and tomato

Snack: Roasted almonds

Dinner: Baked salmon with roasted Brussels sprouts and quinoa

DAY 15:
Breakfast: Veggie omelet with spinach, mushrooms, and red bell pepper

Snack: Rice cakes with peanut butter and sliced banana

Lunch: Tuna salad lettuce wraps with cucumber and tomato

Snack: Grapes

Dinner: Gluten-free spaghetti with turkey meatballs and marinara sauce

DAY 16:
Breakfast: Gluten-free waffles with sliced strawberries and whipped cream

Snack: Hard-boiled egg

Lunch: Grilled chicken Caesar salad with gluten-free croutons

Snack: Roasted pumpkin seeds

Dinner: Baked chicken with roasted sweet potato and green beans

DAY 17:
Breakfast: Smoothie with almond milk, banana, spinach, and peanut butter

Snack: Apple slices with almond butter

Lunch: Turkey and avocado sandwich on gluten-free bread with mixed greens and tomato

Snack: Sugar snap peas with hummus

Dinner: Grilled steak with roasted Brussels sprouts and sweet potato

DAY 18:

Breakfast: Gluten-free oatmeal with sliced apple and cinnamon

Snack: Carrot sticks with ranch dressing

Lunch: Greek salad with mixed greens, cucumber, tomato, and feta cheese

Snack: Trail mix

Dinner: Slow cooker beef chili with gluten-free cornbread

Day 19:

Breakfast: Scrambled eggs with diced bell pepper and gluten-free toast

Snack: Plain Greek yogurt with blueberries and honey

Lunch: Grilled chicken salad with mixed greens, cherry tomatoes, and cucumber

Snack: Roasted almonds

Dinner: Baked salmon with quinoa and roasted asparagus

DAY 20:
Breakfast: Smoothie with almond milk, banana, spinach, and chia seeds

Snack: Rice cakes with peanut butter and sliced banana

Lunch: Turkey and avocado lettuce wraps with cucumber and tomato

Snack: Baby carrots with hummus

Dinner: Stuffed bell peppers with ground turkey, brown rice, and tomato sauce

DAY 21:
Breakfast: Gluten-free pancakes with fresh berries and sugar-free syrup

Snack: Hard-boiled egg

Lunch: Grilled chicken salad with mixed greens, cherry tomatoes, cucumber, and balsamic vinaigrette

Snack: Apple slices with almond butter

Dinner: Slow cooker beef and vegetable soup

DAY 22:

Breakfast: Smoothie with almond milk, spinach, banana, and almond butter

Snack: Rice cakes with hummus and sliced cucumber

Lunch: Grilled salmon with roasted vegetables

Snack: Roasted pumpkin seeds

Dinner: Turkey chili with gluten-free cornbread

DAY 23:

Breakfast: Scrambled eggs with diced bell pepper and gluten-free toast

Snack: Sugar snap peas with ranch dressing

Lunch: Tuna salad with mixed greens, avocado, and cherry tomatoes

Snack: Roasted almonds

Dinner: Grilled chicken with roasted sweet potato and green beans

DAY 24:

Breakfast: Gluten-free oatmeal with sliced apple and cinnamon

Snack: Rice cakes with almond butter and banana slices

Lunch: Greek salad with mixed greens, cucumber, tomato, and feta cheese

Snack: Trail mix

Dinner: Baked salmon with quinoa and roasted asparagus

DAY 25:
Breakfast: Smoothie with almond milk, spinach, banana, and chia seeds

Snack: Hard-boiled egg

Lunch: Turkey and avocado sandwich on gluten-free bread with mixed greens and tomato

Snack: Carrot sticks with hummus

Dinner: Slow cooker beef stew with carrots, celery, and sweet potatoes

DAY 26:
Breakfast: Gluten-free waffles with sliced strawberries and whipped cream

Snack: Apple slices with almond butter

Lunch: Grilled chicken Caesar salad with gluten-free croutons

Snack: Roasted almonds

Dinner: Baked chicken with roasted Brussels sprouts and sweet potato

DAY 27:
Breakfast: Smoothie with almond milk, spinach, banana, and peanut butter

Snack: Sugar snap peas with ranch dressing

Lunch: Tuna salad lettuce wraps with cucumber and tomato

Snack: Roasted pumpkin seeds

Dinner: Gluten-free spaghetti with turkey meatballs and marinara sauce

DAY 28:
Breakfast: Scrambled eggs with sautéed spinach and mushrooms

Snack: Rice cakes with peanut butter and sliced banana

Lunch: Grilled chicken salad with mixed greens, cherry tomatoes, cucumber, and balsamic vinaigrette

Snack: Baby carrots with hummus

Dinner: Stuffed bell peppers with ground turkey, brown rice, and tomato sauce

DAY 29:

Breakfast: Gluten-free oatmeal with sliced banana and almond milk

Snack: Rice cakes with almond butter and banana slices

Lunch: Turkey wrap with gluten-free tortilla, avocado, lettuce, and tomato

Snack: Roasted almonds

Dinner: Grilled shrimp with zucchini noodles and tomato sauce

DAY 30:

Breakfast: Smoothie with almond milk, spinach, banana, and chia seeds

Snack: Apple slices with almond butter

Lunch: Grilled chicken salad with mixed greens, cherry tomatoes, and cucumber

Printed in Dunstable, United Kingdom